Impossible Place

Finding the space you can finally let go

Inspired by a True Story

Merri-jo Hillaker

Sam —

What a breath of fresh air you are to me !__ and many others as well !! Hope you enjoy the book — thank you for it — forward,

JoJo

Quantity sales special discounts are available on quantity purchases by corporations, associations, and others. For details, contact the publisher at the address above.

Orders by U.S. trade bookstores and wholesalers. Email info@BeyondPublishing.net

The Beyond Publishing Speakers Bureau can bring authors to your live event. For more information or to book an event contact the Beyond Publishing Speakers Bureau speak@BeyondPublishing.net

The Author can be reached directly at BeyondPublishing.net

Manufactured and printed in the United States of America distributed globally by BeyondPublishing.net

BEYOND
PUBLISHING

New York | Los Angeles | London | Sydney

ISBN Softcover: 978-1-952884-40-5

Table of Contents

Love always,
Merri-jo Hillaker

Preface

This is an impossible book about an impossible place.

Almost 20 years ago, my brother and father of two children was killed by a bullet from his wife at his place of work.

The murder made headlines and shattered my heart.

I am going to open up to you about what happened to me in the days and weeks that followed.

You need to know that I am a Jesus follower. You also need to know that nothing I had learned or read about God and love and Jesus could have prepared me for the terrifying place in which I found myself. It was a completely impossible place.

I will tell you more about my brother at the end of our story. I want you to know a little bit about him and the wonderful man and friend he was to so many, and the brother he was to me.

But right now, we have other things to talk about. Many of you are living in the impossible place. The need to forgive the unforgivable. I understand. I found myself in the same place.

There is a way out. There is a path forward that can light your way. It will, perhaps, require you to reach past your Sunday school stories into a place you never dreamed possible. This is the big stuff, and you will need to release most of what you thought you knew. The impossible place has its own oxygen and order. I can show it to you from a distance. You will determine what you do with what you discover.

In the Gospel of Matthew, the writer says "with man, this is impossible. With God, all things are possible."

Jesus taught his most important lessons in stories. Like Jesus, I have hidden the truth about the impossible place in the story that follows. I pray that you find your peace.

Merri-jo Hillaker

August 22, 2020

Chapter 1

*"Make us know the shortness of our life that
we may gain wisdom of heart."*
Psalm 90

It had been two years, three months, one week, and five days since Susanne Robbins had last seen her son, Travis, and hugged him in her arms when he surprised her with a visit. Two years, two months, and two weeks since he'd called her on the phone to wish her a happy birthday. Two years, two months, and fifteen days since a police officer arrived on her doorstep to tell her that there had been a hit-and-run accident, and Travis would never be calling or visiting again.

"Alright, thank you, Eleanor, that was a lovely story about your brother," Dr. Elise Abrams said with a gentle smile. Susanne shook herself back to the room and eyed the woman who was leading her group grief counseling session. Dr. Abrams was a beautiful thing with skin the color of coffee and hair twined and braided into an elaborate bun on top of her head. She always dressed in soothing earth tones, with a jangle of bracelets on each wrist that moved musically when she lifted her hands to clap. "Does anyone else have an experience they want to share with the group before we take a break?"

Susanne glanced around the circle, hoping for a volunteer. Most of the members were elderly widows or widowers, with one or two members who had lost a sibling or close friend. Still, at forty-five, she felt like an outsider in the sea of grey hair and glasses. Susanne, by contrast, was a petite woman with mouse-brown hair that she either wore loose or held back with a clip. She'd quit her job as a schoolteacher after Travis's death, but she still dressed like one by wearing comfortable dress shoes, slacks, and conservative blouses. She fidgeted with a simple chain she wore on her wrist—a birthday present from Travis. Why didn't someone stand up? Was she the only one left?

"Thank you, Gail." Dr. Abrams smiled as a plump, cheery-looking woman in a vivid pink shirt and jeans got to her feet. "You have something to share?"

"Well," Gail looked around shyly, "as you know, I lost my husband, Charlie, five years ago, and…" Gail paused, her bright smile wavering for a second. "There have been difficult times to be sure. But today…I was cleaning out a couple boxes in the attic, and I found this…" she dug into her purse and pulled out a faded photograph of a beaming couple in evening dress. "This was a photo we took on our tenth anniversary, and as you see, we're dressed very nice." There were a few chuckles from around the circle. "You see, that night Charlie surprised me with tickets to see *The Magic Flute*, which was my favorite opera. To this day, I still don't know how he was able to afford to take me, but…" Gail looked at the photo fondly. "I just remember finding the photo, and a feeling of… pure joy washed over me, and it took me a minute to realize I wasn't feeling sad." Gail looked around at the group. "You know, two years ago, I would've bawled my eyes out if I'd found this photo, but today, I was able to look at the photograph and…while I felt a little sad, I also felt a sense of peace and happiness. I was able to recall that wonderful memory of my husband and just appreciate that night as a wonderful past experience."

She looked at Dr. Abrams for approval. "I still miss my husband terribly. Charlie was a wonderful man, a wonderful father to our children, and there are days when I feel like I'm missing a limb, but…I'm able to manage better, and I'm so grateful to you, Dr. Abrams, for helping me get to this point."

"You should give yourself some credit, too," Dr. Abrams said gently as everyone else clapped, "and appreciate the progress you've made over the last couple years on your own."

She makes it seem as if grief is merely a phase one can get over with time, Susanne thought bitterly as the group got up and migrated to the refreshment table, where there was store-bought coffee and cookies. How could she forget such an integral part of her soul like her only son? While Gail described missing her husband like missing a limb, Susanne felt as if her entire chest had been torn out and she had been left to bleed. Everyone else had lost their loved one due to age or illness, with plenty of time to say goodbye. Travis had been ripped from her arms at the whim of a drunk driver who hadn't seen the red light.

Susanne had remembered in her grief-stricken state hearing that the driver had been apprehended a few days later, as a traffic camera had gotten a good view of the car as it careened away. Not that it mattered. It wouldn't bring back that beautiful boy who had started to become a man. There had been a trial, and the driver had been sentenced to fifteen years for manslaughter. That had almost been laughable. The court had thought fifteen years was a fair trade for her son's life? Fifteen years was enough time to erase his existence on Earth. She had screamed and raged at that and wished she had been in charge of the punishment. That would've been fairer, right? To let the mother be in charge of his murderer's punishment? If she'd been in charge, she would've done everything in her power to get that driver sentenced to the electric chair. She would've seen that killer strapped into the chair and pushed the kill switch herself.

No one understands the pain I feel, Susanne decided, plastering a fake smile on her face as she sipped terrible coffee and ate the bland pastry. She envied the group as they wandered around, chatting easily with each other and looking like they didn't have a care in the world.

A new face from across the room caught her eye. It belonged to a pretty woman of about thirty, dressed in what looked like a vintage sweater of dark green and matching pencil skirt; her auburn hair curled into old-fashioned ringlets. She caught Susanne's questioning gaze and smiled gently. Susanne looked away. *Probably someone who had walked into the wrong room.*

Susanne waved a half-hearted good-bye to the other members of her group as she left the Recreation Center and ran to catch the bus that would take her to the graveyard. *At least I won't have to do this commute much longer*, she thought as she gratefully sank onto a window seat. A flash of green caught her eye as she relaxed, and she jumped as she saw the strange woman sitting three seats behind her, reading a worn book. She looked even more peculiar than before with her vintage hairstyle and wardrobe. Maybe she worked at some retro-themed shop or restaurant, Susanne guessed. She quickly looked out the window as the woman looked up from her book with a smile.

Susanne got off the bus at her stop, walking quickly toward the cemetery. She glanced back twice, but there was no one behind her.

Susanne placed a bouquet of bright yellow daisies by her son's headstone. "Hello, my darling," she said softly, brushing away a small pile of leaves that cluttered the monument. "I brought your favorites." Travis had loved these flowers growing up. When he was little, he had told her they were like little suns. Little suns for my son, she thought, but even the old play on words that she had said for every special event; championship baseball games, science fairs, school plays, celebratory dinners, every time he made honor roll, meant nothing now. Her son, Travis, the light of her life, was gone now, and the world seemed drab and grey without him.

She eyed the other bouquet of flowers on the grave. They were red and white carnations, and there was a signed baseball tucked next to it.

"Your father said he dropped by to see you last week," she said, picking up the baseball. The signature was from Mike Trout, her son's favorite Angels player. "Believe it or not, that was one of the first civil conversations we've had in years." Susanne had divorced Travis's father, Mark, more than ten years ago. "Turns out, all that was needed to show us how petty our fights were, was to have the most important thing we had ripped out of our lives." She laid her forehead on the cool, marble headstone, and felt a tear run down her cheek. "I know I've said it before, my darling, but while your father and I made many mistakes over the years, you were the most miraculous thing we ever did together."

Tears were flowing down her face now, smudging her make-up, but she didn't care. She suddenly felt older than her forty-five years—old and tired of this miserable world. What did she have to live for, now that her son was gone?

A year ago, she'd had an emotional break-down, coupled with a series of panic attacks, and the doctor had prescribed Valium for her nerves. She'd had one or two, then hoarded the bottle away. She'd slipped the pills in her purse, along with a small flask of alcohol. Everything had been taken care of before she'd left the house. Her assets, her finances, her belongings all in order and detailed in a letter she'd left on the kitchen table, so there would be no muss, no fuss.

Originally, when she thought about ending her life, she'd planned to buy a gun. But that would leave a mess by Travis's grave, and she disliked the idea of some family running into her after she was gone. This way was much better. A quick swig and a swallow, and she could fall blissfully asleep next to her son, and never have to wake up again.

Susanne shook the entire bottle of pulverized Valium into a small glass and poured the contents of the flask in with it. She took one last look around the graveyard as the powder dissolved. It was so peaceful here, with weathered monuments shaded by sweeping trees of various sizes, green grass dotted with clover, and a few birds singing in the trees. She sighed and smiled. She couldn't have picked a better place to die. Now, she could just drift gently off into nothing.

She lifted the glass to her lips…and a child's wailing lament shattered the peaceful silence.

Susanne lifted her head, feeling slightly irritated.

Everyone was entitled to make a certain amount of noise when they lost a loved one, but darn it, right now she was in the middle of something, and she couldn't drift off into serenity if someone was crying in the background.

She waited for a few minutes, hoping the child would quiet down. After a while, the wails of anguish settled into silence.

Susanne lifted the glass to her lips again, and a strong breeze shook the tree, cascading leaves and petals down on her. She glared at the large, sweeping jacaranda tree above her. The branches were filled with purple blooms and the fallen flowers had created a carpet of rich, deep color.

"Would you mind?" she asked sarcastically. There was a petal in her drink, and she took it out and tossed it aside. What did it matter at this point if her drink was a little dirty? Once more, she raised the glass up to her mouth.

There was a flash of green, and suddenly the strange woman was kneeling beside her, her hand on Susanne's wrist.

"Wait," she said, in a pleading voice, and Susanne jerked away, irritated. What was with all these interruptions? Couldn't the world see she wasn't interested in staying?

"Can't you see I'm in the middle of something?" she snapped.

"This is not your time," the woman insisted.

"Says who?" Susanne scowled, feeling like a child on the verge of a temper tantrum. "It's my life, isn't it?" When the woman didn't move, Susanne's temper rose. "Leave me alone!" she said louder, reaching out a hand to shove the woman away. She stopped, mid-push, her mouth gaping in astonishment. For instead of pushing the strange woman back, Susanne's hand had passed right through her... as if she wasn't even there.

Chapter 2

"The sunrise shall visit us from on high to give light to
those who sit in darkness, and in the shadow of death,
to guide our feet into the way of peace."
Luke 1:79

"Stop following me!" Susanne stopped at on the steps of her small condo and glowered at the woman who stood placidly on the path behind her. Dressed in a vintage green suit, her hair in a complicated old-fashioned hairdo, she looked out of place in the suburban neighborhood. "I didn't go through with it, so you can just go back to whatever person you report to and tell them you did your job."

"My work here is not finished, Susanne," the woman said calmly, clasping her hands in front of her. Susanne took a step closer to her door, digging for her keys.

"How do you know my name?" she asked nervously. Susanne wasn't willing to accept this strange apparition was an angel or spirit yet, but on the other hand, it seemed like Susanne was the only one who could see her. More than once on the bus ride home, she'd seen people brush past the vintage-looking woman without seeming to see her, as if the strange woman wasn't there at all. There was a good chance that Susanne was the only one who could interact with her, which meant that either the woman was a vision of unknown origins, or Susanne was losing her mind. She wasn't willing to gamble on which was more likely.

"You have nothing to be afraid of, Susanne," the woman said calmly. "I am merely here to help you, and then I will be on my way."

"Alright, fine." Susanne walked back down the steps to face the strange woman, crossing her arms across her chest. "What do I have to do to get you to go back to wherever you came from?"

"It's time to make peace with your son's death and the driver who caused it," the woman said quietly.

A laugh that Susanne didn't know that she had in her came burbling up and out of her chest.

"Never, never going to happen," she gasped after a few minutes. "All I have left is my anger and the hurt. My son is gone." Tears of mirth were running down her face, or was it grief?

"Then, I will stay to help you until you do," the woman answered.

"You might want to pitch a tent on the lawn then," Susanne wiped the tears from her eyes and fished her keys out of her pocket. "You're going to be waiting a long time."

She unlocked the door to her house and slipped inside, leaving the woman outside and bolting the door securely behind her.

The silence of the empty rooms mocked her as Susanne tossed her keys into a dish by the coatrack, kicked her shoes off, and tossed her jacket on the hook. Shuffling in her socks to the kitchen, Susanne put a kettle of water on the stove and turned on the burners.

The neat stack of documents next to her suicide note were on the table where she'd left them that morning.

Susanne had felt such a sense of relief when she organized her files before she left, put everything in tidy piles for whoever came to her house after her suicide. Soon, she'd told herself, soon she wouldn't have to wake up with the horrible feeling of grief clawing a hole in her chest. Soon, she wouldn't have to find ways to occupy her days, to keep moving forward when all she wanted to do was curl up in a ball and cry. Soon, she could sleep and never wake up again. And even though there was a possibility she might not be reunited with her son, she hoped that at the very least, she'd find peace in death.

Discouraged, Susanne picked up her neatly typed suicide note, crumpled it into a ball, and tossed it in the recycling bin. Thanks to the strange woman who had interfered, her peace would have to wait.

An endless existence of grey, grief-filled days, and a life without her son stretched out before her. Susanne fought back the urge to scream in frustration and instead, took down a box of her favorite tea and the "I Love Mom" mug that Travis had painted for her when he was five.

"I'd like some tea, too, if you don't mind," said a voice from behind her.

Susanne shrieked and dropped the mug on the floor. It shattered, pieces flying over the tiles, as Susanne whirled to face the strange woman who was standing in her kitchen.

"How-how did you…?" she demanded. Her heart was galloping madly in her chest. With any luck, she'd have a heart attack.

"How am I here?"

Susanne nodded dumbly, still shaking.

"I am not bound by the limitations of your world," the woman answered, with a smile.

"Well, that's still not a good enough reason to go barging into people's houses and…" Susanne winced as she stepped on one of the broken pieces of pottery. "Oh no," she whispered, her eyes filling with tears as she crouched to tenderly gather up all the pieces. "No, no, no. This can't be broken; it can't." She'd treasured that mug ever since she'd opened up the gift-wrapped box on Mother's Day all those years ago. Now that she would never see the smiling face of her son again, it was priceless. She clutched the pieces to her chest, rocking as tears spilled down her cheeks. "No, I can't lose anything else from you, Travis."

"Susanne." The woman was kneeling by her side. "I am here to help you."

"Really?" Susanne managed a watery laugh at the strange vision. Maybe she was going insane. Imagining old-fashioned women appearing in her kitchen was probably nothing new. "I don't know how you're helping, but if you fail this job, you'd make a great stalker."

"Listen to me!" the woman demanded. "I am here to be…" She cocked her beautiful head and chose her words carefully. "You can consider me a guide." She nodded, satisfied. "Yes, a guide to help you on the road to forgiveness."

"You're going to help me on the road to forgiveness?" Susanne found herself laughing again. "You are aware that helping me do any form of reconciliation is impossible, right? I'm never going to forgive the monster who took my son away from me."

"The one who sent me has faith that you will find acceptance, and in doing so, you will find peace as well."

"Why would they care about what happens to me?" Susanne scoffed.

The woman reached for Susanne's hand. Almost unconsciously, she expected it to be icy cold, but instead, it was gentle and warm, like a ray of sunshine resting on her fingers.

"You are loved, more than you can possibly imagine." The woman said adamantly. Susanne looked up to meet her gentle, green eyes.

"I'm loved?" Susanne asked.

The woman nodded.

"By the person who ordered you to keep me from dying?"

Another nod. Susanne felt anger, rising like a bitter bile in throat, as she struggled to contain her temper.

"Then why, if they loved me so much, did they not save me from this grief by protecting *my son*?"

The shards of Travis's mug cut into her hands as she sobbed, her shoulders heaving as wave after wave of sadness and anguish threatened to overwhelm her.

"Susanne." The woman was still kneeling at her side. "I can't give you the answer to that question-"

"Of course you can't!" Susanne howled. "You're only good at following people and sticking your nose into their business! Why couldn't you just let me die?" She asked as her tears slowed. "Why was I sent a guide to help me find peace in this life when I am so tired of living?" She wiped roughly at her eyes. "And why am I even talking to you? How do I know you're not a figment of my imagination? I mean, no one else can see or hear you. I can't even touch you."

"Perhaps a quick demonstration would help." The woman sighed and closed her eyes. The shards of the mug in Susanne's hands twitched, and then, as if by some miracle, resolved themselves into one whole piece, the intact mug levitating down to rest gently on the tile floor.

Susanne reached out a hand and gingerly touched the handle. It seemed to be fixed—no, more than that—it looked as if the mug had never been broken in the first place. She turned her astonished gaze to the woman sitting across from her. *No*, she corrected herself, her *guide*.

"How did you do that?" she asked wonderingly.

"As I said," the woman calmly replied, "I am not bound by the limitations of your world." The woman smiled. "It is my intention for you to see beyond what you believe to be true, to see beyond this world as well, in order to see that while something may seem to be broken, it is still possible to return it to its state of original wholeness."

"You're going to teach me how to fix broken mugs?" Susanne asked skeptically.

"In a sense," the woman continued to smile. "I fix broken hearts. I am going to show you the peace and wholeness that still exists within you at your core, the peace you are so desperately looking for."

Susanne hesitantly touched the mug again, trying to reassure herself of its solidity. The woman in front of her might be insubstantial, and possibly be a figment of her imagination, but the mug was not.

"So you fix broken mugs, walk through walls, and you want tea?" Susanne asked, hoping for more of an explanation. "Why?"

"As I said, I am no longer governed by the rules of this world." The woman said. "And I have always loved tea. Do you have Earl Grey?"

"So long as it doesn't go through you and end up on the floor," Susanne said, getting to her feet and taking another mug from the cabinet. Retrieving a box of Earl Grey, she dropped a tea bag into the woman's mug and a bag of chamomile into her own.

The tea kettle was boiling, and Susanne poured hot water into both, and set the mugs on the kitchen table.

"Sit if you like," Susanne said, taking a seat and gesturing to the chair opposite hers. "Or were you planning to hover?"

"I can sit." The woman sank down on the seat.

"To be clear." Susanne said bluntly, "I'm not saying that by giving you tea I'm allowing you to guide me to reconciliation, help fix me, or however you said it."

"Return you to your original state of wholeness," the woman supplied.

"Right." Susanne took a sip of her own tea. " But I want more about who sent you and why you're here."

"You are not able to understand who sent me yet," the woman looked somewhat regretful. "Or what."

"Why?" Susanne demanded.

"You are not empty enough to understand it yet," she shrugged.

"Okay." Susanne shrugged off the prickle of irritation. She felt drained after crying, but the tea was helping to soothe her nerves. "But if I get to that place you are talking about, you'll tell me, right?"

"I won't have to," the woman smiled serenely. "You'll know."

"Fantastic." Susanne muttered into her mug. "Again, this is the same person who wanted you to stop me from killing myself?"

The woman nodded. "It was not your time. It is now. I have been sent to instruct you on your path to peace."

"Which I can attain by forgiving the person who murdered my son." Susanne took a deeper gulp of tea. "So, what do I call you? My guide? Spiritual advisor on the path to forgiveness?"

"Either works." The woman shrugged complacently.

"Don't you have a name?" Susanne asked. "I mean, were you always a guide, or did you ever-"

"Was I ever alive?" The woman nodded. "Yes, I experienced a human life some time ago."

"When was it?"

Susanne's guide frowned, thinking. "1905 to 1945, I believe."

"And what was your name while you were…experiencing human life?"

The woman cocked her head thoughtfully. "It's been so long," she murmured. "Things tend to get a little fuzzy once you become a spiritual guide." She wrinkled her nose, and her eyes lit in recollection. "Ah yes, I remember now. Esther." She nodded in confirmation. "You may call me Esther."

Chapter 3

"Many are the plans in a man's heart,
but it is the Lord's purpose that prevails."
Proverbs 19:21

"A bit much to take in. Where are your wings? Do you have to earn them? I don't recall hearing any bells."

Esther looked away from the car window. "No," she said with a smile. "I don't need to earn my wings. I am already in a state of harmony and aligned with the highest good."

"Does that mean you already have wings hidden away somewhere? Or do spiritual guides not get wings?"

"It means I could appear in front of you without wings if I wanted to. I didn't feel they were unnecessary," Esther said with a laugh.

"Well, I don't know about that," Susanne protested. "Maybe I would've thought I was less crazy if I could see wings or something."

"I have found a fairly normal human form is usually the best approach to start off with."

"Then why are you wearing that old-fashioned outfit?" Susanne asked.

Esther looked down at her well-tailored green suit. "I like this outfit," she replied. Susanne decided to change the subject.

"So, you're just here because someone asked you to." Susanne kept her eyes on the road, despite her overwhelming desire to look at her spiritual guide in the passenger seat. "You're here out of the goodness of your heart? There's no obligation attached?"

"No obligation whatsoever. I am already living in a constant state of bliss. I am good," Esther answered. "There is no need to be feel obligated for any reason. You were in need of assistance, and I was eager to be a part of your human experience."

"And you're still not going to tell me who asked you to help me?" Susanne demanded.

"You may know in time," Esther replied serenely. "Perhaps. Maybe. Can't guarantee it. Possibly. Hard to say."

Her calm, all-knowing state was a bit irritating, Susanne decided. She was hoping she wouldn't have to put up with it for too much longer.

"Assuming that there is any truth to this at all, do you remember anything specific about your human experience?" she asked, changing the subject again.

Esther cocked her head thoughtfully.

"Bits and pieces, yes. I grew up in a good family. I went to school. I was married to a good man who…let's see…he was a jeweler, I believe, so I was able to have a good life for many years. I was also a mother."

"You had children?" Susanne looked at her guide, feeling a little more connected to her.

"I had a daughter, yes." Esther's smile warmed. "A lovely little girl, full of energy and laughter."

"What was her name?" Susanne asked.

"Ilsa." Esther recalled. "My husband named her after his grandmother."

"My husband convinced me to name our son after Randy Travis." Susanne chuckled. "Our first date was at one of his concerts, and we both loved listening to his music. It's one of the few things we both still enjoy." She sighed and shook her head. "A clear sign of an awful marriage, right? The only thing we both loved was Randy Travis and our son."

"On the contrary," Esther said gently, "those seem to be wonderful things to have in common. Your son was very blessed to have such loving parents."

"There were so many things I was looking forward to," Susanne murmured. "I wanted to see him graduate from college, get married— he was dating this lovely girl," Susanne said wistfully. "I wasn't sure if she was the one, but I was still looking forward to his wedding day. And the birth of his children, watching them grow up…" She turned slightly towards Esther. "Were you able to watch any of those milestones with your daughter? I did the math; you passed away when you were forty years old, but—"

"Ilsa's human experience ended shortly before mine," Esther replied. "She was sixteen years old."

"What? How? Why?" Susanne asked, horrified. "Wait, you were alive during World War II. Was your house destroyed during an attack? Or did she get caught during a raid? I know the United States built bomb shelters for that purpose, but—"

"I was not an American citizen during my human experience," Esther interrupted. "My family and I lived in our house in Germany up until…" she paused again, frowning. "1943. After that…" she frowned, her nose scrunching as she tried to remember. "There was a lot of darkness. And cold."

Munich, Germany, 1937

Esther walked home from the store, a heavy bag of groceries under each arm. *De Führer*'s will was being followed wherever she looked, youths with blond hair wore their uniforms proudly, and flags waved from every building. Esther frowned when she came to a shop that used to sell flowers. Usually, the place was occupied by a cheery man and his plump wife, but today, that shop was still and quiet. More and more shops were closing down due to *de Führer*'s decree to shut down *Juden* stores, which made Esther's trip to the market twice as long, since the places she regularly went to were closed.

She saw more and more women were choosing to bleach their dark locks in order to present a safe hair color. Esther had thought about following the trend, but the little vain part of herself had to admit that she didn't want to change her look. She loved her glossy red curls that stood out in the sea of blonde heads, a red rose in a field of daffodils. Even if it made some of *de Führer*'s officers look at her suspiciously, she couldn't bear to change it, even for the sake of blending in.

"Mama!" Little Ilsa, dressed in her crisp BDM uniform, waved from the entrance of her school. Attired in a blue skirt, blouse, and marching shoes, her *safe* blonde hair tied in two pigtails, she crossed the street, her blonde hair bouncing on her shoulders. She threw her arms around her mother the second she reached the other side, her green eyes sparkling as only a ten-year-old's eyes can.

"Hello, darling." Esther stooped to kiss the top of her head. "Be a good little soldier and help your mother with these groceries." She passed her daughter a bag, and Ilsa took it obediently. It seemed her BDM training was really improving her, Esther thought delightedly as they walked down the street. Esther and her husband, Wilheim, had signed their daughter up for *Bund Deutsher Mädel* (Band of German Maidens) when she turned ten, three months ago.

The program was the girl's version of Hitler Jugend, Bund Deutsher Aberiterjugend (Hitler Youth), and promoted physical activities, such as running track, javelin throwing, gymnastics, and camping. Ilsa had gone on three overnight trips so far, and she'd come home with stories of exploring, hiking, and meeting other girls dedicated to the Great Cause of *de Führer*.

Ilsa also learned cooking, sewing, and other important tasks needed in order to run a household. Esther particularly appreciated that Ilsa was learning the importance of obedience, since it meant that her whining and grumbling daughter never had to be told twice to do a chore anymore.

"How was school today, darling?" Esther asked as they made their way home.

"A few more kids in my class are gone," Ilsa said sadly. "Some of the boys were whispering that they were taken away in the middle of the night, then the teacher told them to hush and not talk about it."

More and more people were leaving, Esther thought worriedly. Or worse, people who had displeased *de Führer* were disappearing in the night. Last month, she had begged her husband, Wilheim, to consider packing up his jewelry shop and relocating near her sister's family in Poland. But he had been so stubborn.

"Why should we leave?" He'd laughed. "Business is doing well, I have more and more rich clients every day, and Ilsa is enjoying her school and BDM activities. Do you really want to uproot the family because of a few rumors?"

Not that Wilheim, with his safe blond hair and blue eyes, ever had to worry about being arrested. But more and more people were disappearing every day, and Esther couldn't help but feel nervous.

"Fräulein Ulga, who was teaching us knitting yesterday, said that those who cannot contribute to a better Germany should be removed, as they are unnecessary."

Esther stopped and stared at her little girl, who smiled at her innocently, seemingly unaware of the awful phrase she had just uttered.

"That's something you learned in BDM, dear?" she asked faintly. Ilsa nodded.

"Everything we do is to make this great nation stronger. Heil Hitler!" She saluted, seeing another girl dressed in the same uniform across the street. A feeling of dread made Esther's stomach turn as she watched the little girl and her brother, also in uniform, salute back.

"Heil Hitler!"

******

Susanne stared at the gates of the Women's State Prison. "I don't want to go in," she mumbled.

Esther smiled serenely. "I will not force you. You do not have to go in today, but this is an essential part of your path to peace."

The night before, Esther had told Susanne that the first step of her journey involved going to the prison where her son's killer was being held and talking to her. Esther had said that she wasn't encouraging Susanne to forgive her, but that would be the final step.

Susanne eyed the beautiful woman, still dressed in her vintage suit.

"But if I go through with this, you'll leave?" she asked.

"I will leave when you ask me to leave," Esther nodded.

The night before, after Esther had vanished into thin air, as Susanne had tried to sleep, she'd come up with a simple and brilliant plan. She would go through with the meeting and tell the woman who had hit her son that she forgave her. And then, once her guide had left, Susanne could jump off the nearest bridge. After all, if Esther had been sent to help Susanne forgive, all she had to do was say a few words, and she was gone. Susanne didn't think Esther had any mind-reading abilities. All she had to do was say "I forgive you," and *poof*, Esther would be gone. Simple.

"Alright, I can do this." Susanne said out loud, pulling the car keys out of the ignition. She opened her car door and stepped outside, into the blistering afternoon heat.

"Are you com-" She turned to see if Esther was getting out of the car. There had been no sound of the door opening and closing, but Esther was standing outside the passenger door, looking calm, collected, and cool, as though she was still in the air-conditioned car. Another example of living outside the world's limitations, Susanne mused.

She locked the car and slung her purse over her shoulder. *I can do this*, she told herself and strode towards the gates, Esther walking by her side.

Chapter 4

*"No trial has come to you but what is human. God
is faithful and will not let you be tried beyond your
strength, but with the trial, he will also provide a way
out, so that you may be able to bear it."*
Corinthians 10:13

"How long is this going to take?" Susanne hissed. "We've been waiting ten minutes."

They were sitting in the detention visiting center, surrounded by other inmates visiting their friends and family. The walls were a peeling beige, and through the barred windows, Susanne saw the sun, burning down on the bare landscape that stretched as far as the eye could see.

"Be patient, good things come to those who wait," Esther said calmly.

"I've been through three metal detectors, had to show my identification to multiple guards—"

"Ms…Robbins?" A prison guard approached her. He was tall and shaven, a massive mountain of a man with a small goatee.

"Yes?"

"Alright, Stevens," he turned to the prisoner he was escorting and began removing her handcuffs. "This is your guest. Remember, no contact, and I'll be watching from over there."

Susanne stared at the petite young woman as she sat down, and the security guard moved a few feet away. She looked like she was in her late teens, early twenties, pale-skinned, with dirty-blonde hair twisted tightly into two braids and a dusting of freckles across her nose. Her eyes were grey, heavily shadowed with dark circles that showed that she didn't get much sleep, and lips that were dry and cracked. If it hadn't been for the prison jumpsuit, the girl could've passed for a college student.

"Excuse me," Susanne called to the guard, "I think there's been some mistake."

"You wanted to visit with Katie Stevens?" The guard asked, looking irritated.

"Well yes…"

"Then there's been no mistake, ma'am."

Susanne gaped in astonishment at the girl sitting across from her. This was the woman who had been behind the wheel in Travis's hit and run accident? This was the monster who had killed her son? But she looked so…young and innocent, staring at Susanne with scared and bewildered eyes.

It doesn't matter, she told herself. Just say the words. Just say the words, and you can leave, and Esther will be out of your hair forever.

"Are you my new lawyer?" Katie asked, looking hopeful.

"How…how old are you, Katie?" Susanne found herself asking.

"I'm twenty," Katie answered.

Twenty. Susanne shook her head in disbelief. So young, and her best years would be spent in jail. She almost felt pity for her. This girl had barely started to live, and yet, her life was already over for her in so many ways.

This is the person who killed your son, said the angry part of Susanne's mind. She remembered that Travis had been almost the same age as the girl—Katie Stevens. He would've been celebrating his twenty-first birthday in spring, if it hadn't been for the person sitting in front of her. *She's still so young,* argued another part of Susanne's mind. Katie wouldn't have even finished a semester at college—if she'd gone to college—before the accident.

Stop thinking! Just say that you forgive her and get out of here! urged the voice in her head.

"What exactly are you here for?" Katie was starting to look apprehensive.

Susanne looked to Esther for help, but she just smiled encouragingly.

"My name is Susanne Robbins." Susanne said, her voice shaky. "My son was Travis Robbins."

Katie's face turned dead white, and she looked like she was about to faint.

"You killed my son," Susanne continued, "but I-I-" *Say it! Say you forgive her!* The voice shouted. Susanne struggled to speak but the words were stuck in her throat. She tried again. "I-I- forgi-" Susanne struggled to breathe—there seemed to be no air, and the walls were closing in on her.

Say it! The voice was shrieking. *Say you forgive her!*

I can't, I can't say I forgive her if I don't mean it.

Susanne struggled to her feet. "I can't do this," she muttered as Katie stared at her in bafflement. She turned to Esther who was watching calmly. "I can't say it. I want to, but—" Susanne grabbed her purse. "I have to go. I NEED to go—now."

She hurried away from the table, and as she approached the exit, the security guard snapped to attention, holding out a hand for her identification.

"You know you have more than an hour left, right, ma'am?" he asked.

"I just need to go now, thank you." Susanne said, thrusting the papers at him.

"Wait! Please wait, Ms. Robbins!" Katie was on her feet. She tried to follow Susanne, but her escort immediately blocked her path. "Ms. Robbins! Please! I want to talk to you!"

"I can't stay, let me out of here." Susanne wasn't sure if she was talking to Esther, the security guard or Katie, who was still shouting pleas, nor did she care. All she knew was she had to get out of this suffocating prison. She barely noticed as she was escorted through the various security checkpoints, only relaxing when she was back under the heat of the burning sun again.

Susanne gulped in the humid air, feeling her heart still racing. Her head still whirling. She strode to her car, unlocked and yanked open the door, and collapsed in the burning interior, barely having enough energy to turn on the car in order to activate the AC.

She hadn't expected Travis's killer to be so young, nor to look so fresh-faced and...innocent. For the past few years, she hadn't cared, hadn't wanted to know what the driver had looked like. It was easier to hate a faceless individual, to focus her grief on some abstract monster. So, she had simply imagined Travis's killer as some vague, humanoid blob, and rather than taking any opportunity to confront Katie Stevens, Susanne had barricaded herself away, refusing to even go to the trial, preferring to remain cocooned in her anguish.

Susanne sighed, and rested herself on the steering wheel. Things had been much simpler before she had entered the jail.

"Did you know?" She didn't even bother to look; she knew Esther was beside her.

"Did I know what?" came the calm answer.

"That I'd fail? That I wouldn't be able to forgive her?" she asked bitterly.

"I was focused primarily on the success of your spiritual quest." Esther said gently. "I *wanted* you to be able to find forgiveness so quickly, I was praying for you to find peace, but it is understandable that—"

"I should've been able to do it." Susanne murmured. "I wanted to say the words, I just couldn't. She was just so…young. But at the same time…" She turned to Esther who was sitting comfortably in the passenger seat.

"You should still be proud of your progress. You have started to face the individual who has brought you so much grief, and at the same time, you are aware of how you feel and cannot express something that is not the truth."

"I really wanted to forgive her just, so you would go away." Susanne found herself admitting.

"One day, you will forgive her, and you will truly mean it." Esther patted her hand, and Susanne felt the touch like a light breeze on her fingers.

"Trust me, I'm going to do it the next time I see her," Susanne decided. "I want you gone as soon as possible. I just need a little time to adjust to the person she actually is, rather than who I thought she was."

"And what kind of a person did you think she was?" Esther asked.

"'Not really a person," Susanne replied, "just some thing."

"Then, you should try and get to know her better." Esther nodded. "True forgiveness comes from love and compassion, and compassion comes from understanding."

"I'll think about it." Susanne muttered, as she backed her car out of the parking lot and drove away from the prison.

Munich, Germany 1941

Esther watched as fourteen-year-old Ilsa sprinted down the track towards the finish line, her slim legs flying, her blonde braids bouncing on her shoulders as she sped ahead of the other girls, the crowd roaring in approval.

"And first place goes to Ilsa—" the rest of the announcer's speech was lost as Esther, her husband Wilheim, and the other spectators leapt to their feet, cheering loudly.

"Go Ilsa!" Esther shouted, and she saw her daughter spot her in the stands and wave.

"That is your daughter?" asked a man and woman sitting next to her.

"That's our little girl," Wilheim said, beaming.

"She seems to be of very good Aryan stock," said the man, "and very popular with her teammates."

Esther looked towards the field again, and saw Ilsa was, indeed, surrounded by uniformed boys and girls, who were all congratulating her on her victory.

"Our son, Christoff, is down there as well," said the woman. "We are lucky that our children can be of such benefit to our great leader."

A blond boy in uniform had approached Ilsa and handed her a gold medal. He said something to her and smiled, something that had Ilsa flushing, then smiling back. The way he was looking at her little girl made chills run down Esther's spine. The noise of the people around her could barely be heard over the beat of her own heart. She was so young, but the way she was smiling at that boy and the way he was smiling back at her…

"Yes, we are very proud of her." Esther was dimly aware of her husband's hand on her shoulder. "She will be of enormous importance to our country for years to come."

"Yes…benefit…country." Esther echoed, but she couldn't take her eyes off her little girl, the sun shining and turning her braids to gold as she laughed at something the boy said.

"Essie?" It was Wilheim, staring at her in concern. "You do not look well. Did you say something?"

"No…darling." She tore her eyes away from Ilsa and smiled at him. "Nothing of importance."

Chapter 5

"For no one is cast off by the Lord forever. Though he brings grief, he also will also show compassion. So great is his unfailing love. For he does not willingly bring affliction or grief to anyone."
Lamentations 3:31-3:33

Munich, Germany 1943

"But I have to go!" Ilsa pouted. "It's required for BDM!"

In the past year, Esther had watched Ilsa blossom into a beautiful young lady, with her mother's delicate features and blonde hair all the way down her back. She stood in the kitchen in her BDM uniform, her long white limbs toned and muscled from athletic activities.

"And I'm saying that I'm not sure you should go." Esther replied. She sat by the stove, her hair tied up in a messy bun, mending Wilheim's socks. "I don't like the idea that you'll be interacting with the boys' camp for three days."

"But all the other girls are going!" Ilsa crossed her arms. "They say it's so much fun! There are outdoor activities, like competitions and games, but we can also go hiking and swimming, and at night there are bonfires and dances!"

"Maybe next year, when you're a little older," Esther said firmly.

"I'm going to complain to troop leader Inga!" Ilsa threatened. "Then you'll have to let me go!"

"I thought your troop leader's name was Bridget." Esther finished one sock, and picked up another.

"She got married two weeks ago," Ilsa rolled her eyes in a condescending manner.

"It's hard to keep track when you get a new troop leader almost every two months." Esther snapped. "Was this one pregnant before she got married, too?"

"We are all doing our part to make this country even greater," Ilsa said, turning on her heel and stomping off, just as Wilheim came home from work.

"What's all the fuss?" he asked, looking baffled.

"Ilsa's upset because I won't let her go on the three-day camping trip," Esther said, picking up a new sock. "I told her she could go when she was a little older."

"I thought all her activities were mandatory," Wilheim said, removing his coat.

"We can tell them she's sick. I don't like the idea of her being around all those boys unsupervised."

"But it's mandatory." Wilheim repeated, looking worried.

"Wilheim." Esther put down the sock and took her husband's hands in her. "Mrs. Geiter, you know our neighbor from down the street? Her daughter isn't much older than Ilsa. Gertie went to one of those three-day camping events, and …" She hesitated. "There was an incident with a few of the officers. Now she's pregnant, and they have no idea who the father is."

"Well," Wilheim shrugged uncomfortably. "You know how young people are sometimes; it's hard to control them."

"I don't want Ilsa to be in such an unsafe environment!" Esther could feel her temper rising.

"Mama," Ilsa stood in the hallway, holding the phone, stretched to the end of its cord. "It's for you."

"Thank you, darling. I didn't even hear the phone ring," Esther said, taking it from Ilsa. "Yes, this is Essie Schatz," she said politely into the receiver. "Who is this?"

"Mrs. Schatz," said the cold female voice on the other end of the line. "This is troop leader Inga. Your daughter tells me that you don't want her to go to the mandatory camp weekend."

Esther's jaw dropped, and she stared at her daughter, who was watching smugly, a look of righteous satisfaction on her face.

"Yes. Well…" she stammered. "I just checked her temperature, and she has a bit of a fever."

"Mrs. Schatz, your daughter mentioned that you would try to lie to us in order to take her out of the event. I should tell you that *de Führer* does not take kindly to deception."

Esther's hands were trembling as they held the phone receiver. "Look… troop leader…" she stammered, "I don't think the excursion will be safe for my daughter. I just want to keep her protected. You can understand that, can't you?"

"Mrs. Schatz." The voice on the other end sounded neither compassionate nor understanding. "Rest assured, your daughter will be supervised by myself and the other troop leaders, who have her best interests at heart. That being said, the camping trip *is* a mandatory trip sanctioned by the *Führer*, and if she does not attend, there will be serious consequences for you and your family. Is that clear?"

"Yes, ma'am." Esther said faintly.

"Heil Hitler," Inga said, and to Esther, it sounded like a reminder.

"Heil Hitler," Esther repeated, and there was the sound of the dial tone as troop leader Inga hung up.

"Who was that?" Wilheim asked.

"Troop leader Inga," Esther's hands were shaking so badly that she almost dropped the phone as she returned it to the hook. "She says Ilsa is required to go on the trip."

"I told you I had to go." Ilsa was still looking infuriatingly smug. Esther glared at the little demon who used to be her sweet, obedient little daughter. "I still don't like the idea."

"Well, if you try and keep me from going, I'll tell the troop leader, and she'll have you thrown in prison, or worse!" Ilsa stuck out her tongue like a child. Esther raised her hand to strike Ilsa, but Wilheim was quicker. His hand slapped Esther's cheek, and she cried out in shock and pain.

"How dare you endanger this family by trying to go against the will of the *Führer!*" He shouted. "You were lucky that it was only a warning this time, what if they had taken us away for defying him?"

"Your daughter is the one who endangered the family by reporting it!" Esther whimpered, holding her cheek.

"I am following the will of the *Führer*, like a true patriot." Ilsa declared, drawing herself up proudly. "If you disobey, you're the traitor! And you deserve to be punished!"

"You would turn in your own mother?" Esther felt the prickle of tears, then flinched as Wilheim raised his hand for another slap.

"Our daughter is right," Wilheim said coldly. "We cannot risk angering our great leader."

* * *

Susanne sat by the side of the road, her head in her hands. The sun was just going down, and it felt like she was the only one out there on the vast, barren highway.

"She was so young," she repeated. "If she hadn't been so young, then maybe I could've said I forgive her."

"Would you have meant it?" Esther asked gently.

Susanne shrugged. "Does it matter? You said you would go when I forgave her."

"But you still would need to mean it," Esther replied.

"You wouldn't have left? You lied to me?" Susanne turned toward her spiritual guide. "You're saying you wouldn't have left, even if I said I forgave her?"

"If you don't mean it, then it's not really forgiveness." Esther stated calmly.

"But...that means I'm stuck with you forever!" Susanne sputtered. "Because I can't- I can never forgive her for taking my son away from me!" She put her face in her hands again, exhausted. "I'm going to be considered the crazy lady for the rest of my life, because I've got some 'spiritual guide' hanging around me that only I can see." Susanne massaged the bridge of her nose. "I should start ignoring you. Like, starting right now, I need to start ignoring you. That way, I can fake the fact that I'm normal."

"Why don't you rest for a little bit, Susanne," Esther kindly suggested.

"I can't hear you," Susanne put her fingers in her ears. "There's no one here; I just have to try and live a normal life alone, because no one understands me."

"I understand you," Esther reminded her quietly.

"You are not real. You're a figment of my imagination. Why am I doing this?" Susanne asked herself. "I can't go through life with my fingers in my ears." She started to dig through the car console, looking for earplugs.

"What would you say if I told you that I could find you some people who would understand you?" Esther asked. "People who are currently dealing with the loss of a child?"

"Esther, I'm not driving all over the state. And even if you do find them, what am I supposed to say? 'Hi, my invisible friend sent me?'" Susanne found a wad of old tissue and tore it in half.

"I could take you to them," Esther said. "Why don't you rest in the meantime?"

"If it's all the same to you, I'm just going to drive home and pretend you're not there…for the rest of my life." Susanne stuffed a piece of tissue in each ear. "Bye now."

"Sleep." Esther reached out and touched Susanne's shoulder. The woman immediately slumped in the driver's seat, snoring.

"You weren't kidding when you said she snores," Esther murmured out loud. "Forgive me for being impatient with her…but this might help her heal before she tries to forgive."

Starting the car, Esther directed it down the open highway, her precious cargo snoring and blissfully unaware.

* * *

Susanne woke up and blearily looked around.

"Wha- where are we?" she asked.

"Arizona," Esther said calmly. Susanne's eyes widened in shock. "We were driving all night long?"

"You needed the rest."

"What part of being a spiritual guide allows you to drive my car across the state?" Susanne shouted.

"You wished to find people who could understand you," Esther replied.

"I'm turning this car around and driving home." Susanne turned the keys in the ignition. The engine sputtered, then died.

"You're out of gas." Esther informed her.

"I'll just call for a tow truck." Susanne pulled out her phone.

"Your battery is also dead." Esther continued calmly.

"ARGH!!" Susanne beat her fists on the dashboard in frustration.

"How about you come inside with me," Esther smiled. "I'm sure someone would be willing to lend you a little gas."

"Or at least show me an outlet that I can use to charge my phone," Susanne sighed, grabbing her purse and getting out of the car.

Esther had parked her next to a church, and Susanne distastefully eyed the building. It was a charming adobe structure with cacti and drought-friendly flowers growing in a rock garden. It looked like a safe haven, epitomizing peaceful serenity. Susanne immediately hated it.

With Esther in tow, Susanne pushed through the wrought-iron gate, and up the three stone steps to the door.

"Hello?" Susanne lifted her hand to knock, but the door opened at her touch. She peeped in. "Hello? Anyone here?" She pushed the door open wider. A murmur of voices could be heard from farther away down the hall.

"You're going to have to go to them," Esther said mildly. "I don't think they know you're here."

"I was going to!" Susanne snapped. *I just want to get this over with*, she thought, and strode down the corridor, towards the sound of the voices. *I just hope these people aren't spiritual guides, too.*

A door halfway down the hallway was open, and she could see a circle of people sitting inside a large room. One woman, a tall, blonde and slender individual in her late fifties was reading something that sounded biblical, though Susanne couldn't place the passage.

"'For God so loved the world, that he gave his only son, that whoever believes in him should not perish, but have eternal life. For God did not send his son into the world to condemn the world, but in order that the world might be saved through him.'" The woman smiled around at the group.

"I realize that not all of us who meet here are Christian or Catholic—or even believe in God, but yesterday I was sitting by the window, thinking about my daughter, Cassie, and…" she paused and seemed to choose her words carefully. "For me, at least, God seemed to be the ultimate parent who would understand what it means to lose a child. Even if no one else could understand the pain I went through when my daughter died, God would, because He had lost his son, too. And that…" she paused again, "that gave me comfort when things were hardest, because I could always pray to Him and know that He had felt the same pain I did—" The woman stopped as she saw Susanne standing in the doorway. The woman's smile brightened, and she stepped forward, one hand out to shake. "Hello," she said, clasping Susanne's hand. "I'm Beth Johnson, the president of this little group. Are you here to join Helping Parents Heal?"

"No, sorry." Susanne shook her head, "my car just ran out of gas, and I was hoping to get some help."

"Of course," Beth nodded. "We are here to give you and your friend all the help you need."

"My—" Susanne turned around to see if there was someone else standing behind Esther, but there was no one. "Are you able to, can you *see* her?"

"Of course," Beth smiled.

"Susanne," said Esther, "Beth is a spiritual medium, as well as being the president of Helping Parents Heal."

"And Helping Parents Heal is what, exactly?" Susanne asked.

"Helping Parents Heal is a support group." Beth explained. "Specifically for parents who have lost their children." Still smiling, she took Susanne's hand and guided her towards the circle. "Why don't you take a seat and join us."

Chapter 6

"We will not fear, though the Earth gives way and the mountains fall into the Sea, though its waters roar and foam and the mountains quake with their surging. The Almighty Lord is with us."
Psalm 46:2-3,7

"Please, here, take a seat," Beth gestured toward an empty chair. "Can I offer you something to eat?" She indicated a table that was furnished with a tray of sandwiches, some fruit and veggie platters, cookies, and bottled drinks.

"No, thank you," Susanne demurred, "as soon as I get some gas, I should start driving back". Her stomach rumbled loudly, interrupting her protests. "Maybe I could stay for a few minutes," Susanne decided. After all, she hadn't eaten for almost twelve hours.

"Help yourself." Beth smiled warmly.

"Thank you," Susanne said, moving over to the table as quickly as possible. Grabbing a plate, she piled it with three sandwiches, a handful of fruit, and a cookie.

"Let me introduce you to the group," Beth said as Susanne took her seat. "Abby and John, Chris and Sierra, Laura and Peter are regular members who are part of our meetings, while Jane, Marcus, Andrea, and Joyce are our founding members, when we were established in 2010."

"Beth is the primary founder, though," Marcus spoke up. He was a handsome man with copper skin and salt-and-pepper hair. "She started the group a few years after the death of her son."

"You lost your son, too?" Susanne looked sympathetically at the quietly composed woman.

"And my daughter. Callie, I lost in childbirth; she was dead before she was born. But my son, David, was twenty-one years old." She smiled sadly. "He was an avid mountain climber, and for his spring break, he and his friends decided to climb Mt. Everest. Halfway up the mountain, his body couldn't take the altitude, and he collapsed. He was dead before they got him back to base camp." Beth wiped away a tear. "I spent quite a few years grieving. What helped me get through it was my network of friends, a few of whom had lost their children as well."

"I was one of those people," Marcus spoke up again. "I lost my son Ian to cancer when he was eleven. Beth would often reach out to me while my wife and I were grieving to make sure we were okay, and when David passed, we extended the same kindness."

"It occurred to me that it might be a good idea to create a group exclusively for parents who needed help dealing with the death of their children," Beth said. "We started off with just a few people, but now we have almost 2,000 members worldwide."

"Beth recruited me to help with organization," Marcus said. "I help co-ordinate group meetings, as well as booking buildings when we have our larger events."

"I'm the finance girl," Andrea spoke up. She was a pudgy woman with thick glasses and black hair. "Sometimes, we hold fundraisers to raise money for cancer research, funeral funds for struggling families, or we need to rent a room for large events."

"How large are these events?" Susanne was curious.

"Sometimes, we can get two to three hundred people," Beth said. "Though now that we've started live streaming, we can reach even more people globally."

"My daughter was hit by a drunk driver when she was only eighteen," Andrea added, "It's been about ten years since she passed."

"My son, Travis, was killed in a car accident as well," Susanne focused on Andrea. "How did you—how do you deal with it?"

"For a number of years, I was angry." Andrea admitted. "My beautiful baby had been taken from me by some stupid idiot, and it seemed like I had been punished for something that I didn't deserve. But…" she continued, "over time, that anger started to take a toll on me. The longer I held onto that hate, the more damage it did to me physically."

"You had every right to be angry," Susanne protested.

"Yes, but…" Andrea stopped. "Have you ever heard of the water glass analogy?"

"Glass half empty or half full?" Susanne asked.

"No," Andrea shook her head. "Beth did a lecture about it a while back. Beth, why don't you tell Susanne about it?"

"Imagine that you have condensed all your anger into a water glass," Beth said serenely, "and you're holding it out in front of you. It's easy at first to hold it out there, it seems like a fairly simple task at first—after all, a glass of water isn't that heavy." Susanne nodded, comprehending.

"But how long can you continue hold it out like that?" Beth asked. "After a while it takes more and more effort, and while you can continue to hold it out there if you put all your muscles into it, after a while, it will begin to damage your body, physically and mentally."

"I don't want to stop being angry." Susanne murmured. "If I do, then how can I justify that I loved my son? How can I let go of his death as if his life didn't matter?"

"Why must you honor his death by being angry and sad for the rest of your life?" Joyce spoke up for the first time. She was a wiry woman with white hair and glasses perched on the edge of her nose. "How is focusing all your energy on hate benefiting anyone?"

"Well, how do you handle their deaths?" Susanne snapped, feeling a little irritated.

"The same way I've dealt with it for the past thirty years and five months, I suppose," Joyce answered calmly. "I just take it one day at the time." She smiled wryly. "Some days are better than others…but that's okay. I think my Ashley and Joshua can understand their mom is only human. On the really hard days, I like to take out a box of family pictures and just…look at them. And that usually gets me through until the next day."

Thirty years. Susanne stared at the woman with a mixture of admiration and respect. "Does it…ever stop hurting?" She looked around at the circle of parents. One by one, they all shook their heads.

"Even after fifteen years, I still think about Ian." Marcus spoke up. "If he was still alive, he'd be twenty-six, so he'd have finished college, and be honing his craft in whatever career he chose." He looked thoughtful. "Ian always loved rocks. He'd go out on these all-day hiking excursions, and come back with his backpack almost twenty pounds heavier, just weighed down with every cool rock he'd found. I like to think that if he was still alive, he'd want to be a geologist, exploring and traveling all over the world to find the one rock that no one had ever seen."

"My daughter was a dancer," Andrea said quietly. "I loved watching her practicing in the backyard. Now, the house is so quiet."

"Ashley wanted to be an astronaut princess, and Joshua wanted to be a pirate," Joyce reflected. "They were only four, though, so a lot more things seemed possible." Susanne actually chuckled, then stopped, feeling guilty.

"Our children are a part of us," Beth said quietly. "Whether it has been a day or fifty years since they left this world, we're still their parents. We will always feel their loss. But I found it was easier to deal with my burden of grief when I was surrounded by others who understood and empathized with my pain."

"Travis was in his third year of college." For the first time, as Susanne shared about her son, she really felt like these people understood. "He still had one year left, but he loved his classes, he loved meeting different people in different programs, he was just enjoying the whole college experience. He was playing baseball, but a few people had tried to get him to do it professionally. He had—" Susanne choked up. "So much potential. Such a bright future ahead of him, and then, suddenly, it was just gone!" She wiped at an errant tear. "I just have to wonder why, why did this happen? What was the point?" Susanne looked around the circle. "We were given such a blessing, and then, it was taken away? Why?"

"We can't answer that question." Andrea had taken Susanne's hand. "We can only try and appreciate the time we were given, the lessons our children taught us, and love them, whether they are on this earth or not."

Beth took Susanne's other hand. "No matter what, you're not alone. No matter what, if you need support, we are here."

More tears rolled down Susanne's face. "I tried to face the driver who hit my son." Another tear fell. "I wanted to talk, I was supposed to forgive her, because…" she indicated Esther, who had been sitting and listening quietly the whole time. "My spiritual guide seemed to think it was important. But I couldn't do it. I was expecting…" Susanne thought back to the young girl in the orange jumpsuit. "Anything but her. She was just so young. I didn't even realize she was the one until the prison guard told me. If I'd seen her on the street, I'd have thought she was a college kid, just like my son, Travis."

"Susanne," Esther spoke, though only Susanne and Beth seemed to hear her. " I never intended to pressure you into giving forgiveness. I only wanted to help you release your anger."

"Instead of focusing on the encounter as a failure, think of it… as a first step." Joyce encouraged her. "You have started by making contact and seeing this person face-to-face."

"So, what's my next step?" Susanne asked.

Beth smiled. "That is up to you."

* * *

Munich, Germany 1943

A mother's nightmare is when her worst fears come true.

Ilsa left for her three-day excursion, eager, cheerful, confident. She came back, reserved, emotional, and brittle. She would not tell Esther what had happened. Instead, she would wake up screaming in the middle of the night. Every time, Esther would rush to her daughter's room, and every time, Ilsa would claw and kick and bite when Esther tried to hold her. Ilsa would not talk about her night terrors. She would not explain why she burned her BDM uniform. She would not say where the bruises on her wrists and ankles came from, but Esther could guess.

"We should never have let her go on that trip," she told Wilheim after she had soothed Ilsa for the third time that night.

"It was the *Führer's* will. Would you rather have defied him and been sent to prison?" He took a swig from the flask beside him. Lately, Wilheim had been drinking heavily, though whether it was out of guilt or fear, Esther couldn't say.

"If it was the *Führer's* will, he should also be expected to deal with the consequences," Esther snapped.

Wilheim slapped her hard. "Be careful what you say." He looked around, eyes wide. "The walls have ears."

Two weeks passed, and Ilsa still refused to leave her room. She ate poorly, slept little, becoming gaunt and thin. Then, on the fourteenth day, troop leader Inga came for a visit. Esther was surprised when she saw her for the first time. Inga was a well-muscled, yet petite woman of twenty. Her eyes were such a dark blue they were almost a dangerous black, but her hair was a safe blonde, though Esther suspected she used a little peroxide to make it lighter. Inga smiled, looking as harmless as a bunny rabbit.

"Good Afternoon, Mrs. Schatz, I came over to see how Ilsa was doing. I missed her from our meetings. You know it is mandatory that she comes—otherwise, your family might face a fine or…" she shrugged. "Worse."

"She has not left her room since the three-day camping excursion." Esther felt rage boiling inside her. "You said that event would be supervised."

"It was, very much so." Inga's smile did not waver. "The recruits seemed to have an enjoyable time."

"How dare you." Esther took a step forward, "my daughter can barely sleep because of nightmares, and you say that she had an enjoyable time?"

"Mrs. Schatz, you must understand. The BDM teaches young women many useful things. Discipline and obedience, pride for our country, how to run a successful household by teaching cooking and cleaning… but we women have a very important role into making this great country stronger that only we can do." She laid a hand on her stomach and her eyes glittered with fervor. "I, myself, am an eager participant in our glorious fight. Though soon, I will have to step down, in order to properly raise the *Führer's* newest recruit and most loyal soldier." Inga tried to step around Esther. "I should talk to your daughter for a little bit. Maybe I can help explain to her the valuable role she will be playing." Esther barred the door.

"You stay away from my daughter," she said coldly.

Inga eyed Esther with distaste. "You should not stand in my way. I am a loyal supporter of the *Führer*, and a member of his beloved Aryan race. You, on the other hand…" She looked Esther up and down, from her hair that was neither brown nor blonde, to her eyes that were too green to be blue, but still dangerous. "You might be better off elsewhere if you continue to stand in my way."

Esther slammed the door in her face. She stood outside for a few minutes, yelling insults, before finally going away. As she turned away from the door, she saw Ilsa standing on the top of the stairs.

"Don't worry, darling, she's gone."

"She told me that it was my privilege to help." She crumpled at the top of the stairs, whimpering. "My honor to aid my country…but it didn't feel like an honor."

"Sweetie," Esther approached her gingerly. "I promise, I will never let her walk into this house, if you never want to see her again."

"Then you'll have to leave." Wilheim was standing in the shadow of the hallway, a bottle in one hand. "I cannot have resisters in my house," he rasped. "I will not disobey the will of the *Führer*. If you stay here, they will drag us all to their camps to die."

"Darling," Esther called up to Ilsa. "Pack your bags, we leave in an hour."

Chapter 7

*"If he sins against you seven times seventy in one day,
and turns to you each time, saying 'I repent',
you must forgive him."*
Luke 17:6

"I didn't think you'd be back," Katie commented as she sat down at the prison visiting center.

"I didn't think so, either," Susanne admitted.

"So…this is your lawyer?" Katie asked, looking nervously at Beth.

"No, just a friend," Beth squeezed Susanne's hand. "I'm here for moral support."

It had been a month since Susanne had met the group, Helping Parents Heal. That day, Susanne had impulsively gotten a hotel room and stayed for a week to attend meetings. But when she did leave, it was with the numbers of all the members on her phone. Out of all of the members, though, Beth was the one Susanne felt closest to. She called Susanne every day, and they spent hours talking, crying, and even laughing. It felt good for Susanne to laugh after so long, but every time she did, she still felt a little guilty, as if she was betraying her son's memory by enjoying herself.

"Why do you feel guilty?" Esther asked after Susanne confided to her. "What is wrong with being happy?"

"But my son is gone, I should be mourning him for the rest of my life," Susanne insisted.

"So, you plan to live your who life without ever laughing again?" Esther asked. Susanne shrugged. "Susanne," Esther continued gently. "Would Travis want you to be unhappy for the rest of your life?"

"Travis…never liked seeing me unhappy." Susanne remembered. "He was always making silly faces, telling me jokes, or giving me a little bouquet of flowers if it ever seemed like I was sad."

"Then, doesn't it seem like you should be allowed to laugh without betraying his memory?" Susanne was silent. "Susanne, remember the glass." Esther advised her. "At some point, it will become more and more difficult to remain unhappy. Why not honor his memory by living the best life you can, and letting go of a few things that make you miserable?"

Susanne sighed. "You want me to go back to the prison, don't you?"

Esther shook her head. "You can go whenever you want, but I think you might be ready."

In the end, Susanne was only willing to go if Beth came with her for emotional support. It had taken a little longer to get approved for a visit, but finally, Susanne was back in that room, talking to the woman who had killed her son.

"So…" Katie took a deep breath. "What did you want to talk to me about?"

"You know who my son Travis is," Susanne started.

"Yes, ma'am." Katie's eyes filled with tears. "He's the man I hit when I was trying to go to the hospital."

Susanne was taken aback by that response. "Hospital? Why were you going to the hospital?"

"Well, ma'am, my water had just broken, and I was going into labor."

"Perhaps, we should start at the beginning," Beth said gently, looking between the two women.

"Well," Katie linked her fingers together. "I didn't have any money for college, so after high school, I started working every job I could get to save up for classes."

"What about your parents?" Susanne was compelled to ask.

Katie shrugged. "My mama died of cancer when I was eight. My daddy… he made enough to look after all of us, but not enough that I could ask him to pay for more school. He still had my two brothers to raise, so I told them I'd earn the money on my own."

Katie sighed. "I was doing pretty well. I'd been working hard for two years. I'd saved enough that I could take classes at a decent school, had a partial scholarship, and it looked like I was going to be on my way toward my goal. I was feeling so good, I went out to celebrate with some friends…and got myself knocked up." Katie smiled wryly. "I'd been doing pretty well until then. My baby's father made it real clear he wasn't interested in being in the picture. And by that, I mean I was never able to contact him after that one night."

"That must've been scary." Beth said. "How did your father react?"

Katie shrugged again. "He was a little disappointed. I think he saw my education dreams as over, now that I had a baby to care for. But he said he'd support us if we needed help." She sighed. "I kept working and saving, but now, I was saving so that I could support my baby when she was born. Kept working right up until I was supposed to go on maternity leave." Katie tugged miserably at one of her braids. Susanne felt a twinge of pity as a tear rolled down Katie's face.

"You don't have to keep going with your story right now—"

"No." Katie shook her head. "I want to finish it." She wiped away the tear. "I was due to give birth in January, but I went into labor two weeks early. I was alone in the house, Daddy had taken my brothers to a football game and couldn't get back for at least two hours. I thought I could make it to the hospital on my own. I got in the car, and just…drove. The contractions were bad, and the roads were icy, because it was the middle of winter, but I didn't think to stop."

Katie put her head in her hands. "I was in so much pain from the contractions, I was just focused on getting there as fast as possible…I didn't see the patch of ice until I hit it. I lost control of the car, it went spinning and I slammed into your son's truck." Katie looked at Susanne, misery written on her face, tears flowing freely. "I'm sorry…I'm so, so sorry…it was an accident. I didn't mean to kill him."

Something inside Susanne was cracking, breaking open. Like a key had found the right lock, and now a door within her could finally open.

My son is still dead. She is still the woman who killed my son, Susanne thought, as she stared at Katie as she buried her face in her hands. *Am I able to look past her deed? She never meant to take him away from me. She's probably spent the last two years suffering more than I have.*

Susanne looked at Katie again. She could let her continue to blame herself. She could walk away and let this woman live with the pain of her mistake for the rest of her life. Susanne remembered what Esther had said earlier that month. *Did she really want to honor his memory by allowing someone else to be miserable? Did Katie deserve to live with the pain?*

She's already suffered enough. Susanne realized. *Only I can help her.*

Susanne reached out a hand to the woman she had blamed for the last two years, five months, and two weeks for the death of her son. Her tears ran down her cheeks from a place very deep inside.

"I believe you. And I forgive you."

Katie stared at Susanne's hand, with a mixture of relief and gratitude on her face, clutched the hand in hers, and wept.

* * *

Munich, Germany 1944

They ran that night, Esther and Ilsa, heading for the safety of Poland under the cover of darkness. They took only the bare necessities of what they could carry, riding on the backs of trucks when they could, walking along the road and hiding when they spotted Nazi troops. With no idea of who they could trust, and who they couldn't, Ilsa and Esther didn't dare approach any of the farmhouses they passed once they were outside the city. Instead, they slept in any barns that looked abandoned, curling up in the hay and stealing what little food they could find.

The months went by, and Ilsa's belly swelled like a watermelon with her unborn child. It became harder and harder to travel more than a few miles in her condition. They rested more often, and Esther fed her any extra sustenance she could find, but still, she became thin and gaunt from lack of food and water, her beautiful blonde hair became drab and tangled, and her blue eyes were always fearful, always searching for danger.

Autumn had come and gone, the leaves turning golden brown and falling, and now winter was upon them. The days and nights became colder, and it was harder to find food now that the ground was covered in frost. Esther prayed every night that they would make it to Poland safely. They were only a week's walk away from the border. If they could manage to survive another week, they would soon be out of Germany and safe from the *Führer*'s oppressive rule.

"Mama, I'm so tired." Ilsa staggered along, her ankles swollen in her battered shoes. "And hungry. I haven't eaten anything all day."

"Keep going, my darling," Esther encouraged her. "I saw a barn up ahead that might do for the night. If we can make it there, you can rest while I find food."

The barn wasn't exactly intact. There were gaping holes in the roof and walls from neglect and looters, but it looked like it had been abandoned for months. So Esther made Ilsa comfortable on a bed of hay and went to find food in the remains of the fields. The ground there was almost frozen, and it looked like there were no vegetables left. Still, Esther dug into the earth, tearing her nails as she searched the clods for something, anything they could eat. Finally, in the farthest corners, she was able to unearth some withered carrots, and a large turnip that was about the size of her hand. Esther staggered back to the barn, her treasures clasped in frozen, bleeding fingers, and placed the food in Ilsa's hands.

"Happy Birthday, darling."

* * *

"Mama!"

Ilsa's whimpers woke Esther in the middle of the night. The metallic stench of blood was thick in the air as she fumbled in the darkness, adding wood to the fire she had made in an old bucket. It took only a look to know Ilsa had miscarried. Ilsa's skirts were soaked in red, and Esther's hands became too, as she labored over her daughter, piling blankets on her to keep her warm. As the moon rose and the icy night froze Esther's fingers, she pulled Ilsa's tiny daughter into the world, wrapping her in a spare piece of cloth and holding the tiny bundle close.

"Mama, let me hold her," Ilsa begged. Esther hesitated, then passed the baby over. She was barely the size of Esther's forearm, but Ilsa took her gently, lovingly in her arms. "Why isn't she crying?" Ilsa asked.

"She's sleeping," Esther lied as her daughter gazed at the tiny face lit by the light of the fire.

"She's beautiful." Ilsa whispered, and kissed the tiny forehead gently.

"Yes, she is." Esther curled up next to Ilsa to give her more warmth. Ilsa was still bleeding heavily. Esther couldn't stop the flow, and the blankets were slowly turning crimson.

"I was thinking about names." Ilsa murmured. She was still shivering, no matter how tightly Esther held her. "What about Gentiana? Doesn't she look like a precious little flower?"

"She does; it's perfect," Esther agreed, kissing her forehead. Gentiana lay still and quiet in her daughter's arms, growing colder and colder as the morning sun rose in the sky. Ilsa was growing colder as well as her blood continued to seep out of her body.

"Mama, I'm so tired," Ilsa murmured, resting her head on Esther's shoulder.

"Then sleep, my darling." Esther continued to hold her close.

"Will you sing us that lullaby you did when I was younger?"

"Of course."

And Esther sang, as the sun rose higher in the sky, holding her daughter and granddaughter in her arms. Ilsa slipped away peacefully, her breath becoming fainter and fainter, until it was no more. *If God is kind*, Esther thought, as she curled up next to her daughter's cold body, *he will take us away from this place together.* But while God was kind to Ilsa, he wasn't kind to her.

Chapter 8

*"Give your burdens to the Lord, and he will take care
of you. He will not permit the Godly to step and fall."*
Psalm 55:22

"What happened to…well, your child?" Susanne asked. She was visiting Katie again, this time alone.

"My daddy was given custody. He brings her by to visit sometimes. She's almost three years old now." She reached for her prison jumpsuit and the prison guard supervising was immediately on alert.

"What you got there, inmate?" He took a few steps towards Katie.

"It's nothing dangerous, I swear," Katie carefully pulled a well-worn picture out of her prison jumpsuit, and held it out to show. The guard relaxed, and returned to his post. Katie held it out to Susanne. It was dirty, and creased, but she could still make out the chubby, dimpled face, smiling and full of innocence and joy.

"She's precious," Susanne cooed over the picture.

"Her name is Lily." Katie said softly. "I've always loved those flowers." She hesitated, then continued. "Daddy tries not so show it, but I can tell that the added burden is difficult on him. Hard to be a grandfather and raise my brothers at the same time." She looked Susanne in the eye. "I know I deserve my sentence, but I'm going to do everything I can to earn my release, so I can raise my little girl. It won't be easy." Katie took back the photo and tucked it carefully into her jumpsuit again. "There won't be a lot of high-class jobs for someone like me, but I'm going to try and make a good life for her, so she can have opportunities that I never will."

Susanne tried to cheer the girl up. "You shouldn't be so hard on yourself."

"Please." Katie waved a dismissive hand. "I know that it's going to be tough. I'm serving a ten-year sentence for manslaughter; I'll be lucky to get a job as a waitress."

"Is there any way you can you get your sentence reduced?"

Since she'd last seen Katie, Susanne had researched everything she could about the case that she hadn't cared about before. She went to city hall and the police station to access all the files she could, and was even able to view the traffic camera that had filmed the whole thing. She'd watched as Katie's car had hit a patch of ice, skidded along the road, the tail-end slamming into Travis's truck, sending it flipping over on its side. In many ways, it felt as if a weight had been lifted off her shoulders. Susanne no longer felt the anger and resentment that she had carried for so long.

It had been an accident. There had been no monster behind the wheel, actively trying to hit her son as he was driving, just a girl who had been scared and was in pain, rushing to get the help she needed.

"I'm doing everything I can to be a model prisoner," Katie was saying. "I'm hoping to have a chance for an appeal soon, maybe that will knock a few years off."

"I could provide a character reference." The words were out instinctively, before Susanne could take them back.

"You'd do that?" Hope shone on Katie's face like a beacon.

"Yes." Susanne nodded. "Look, Katie…I never thought that I'd be here talking with you. For years, the person responsible for my son's death was just a nameless, faceless…entity that had destroyed my life. But you're nothing like what I imagined. I think you have a lot of courage and integrity, to want to raise your daughter alone, and the fact that you plan to do everything you can to give her a better life is admirable. I think you are a genuinely good person, and I think if Travis was still alive, I think he would say the same."

Tears glimmered in Katie's eyes. "Thank you." She took a deep breath. "Would you consider being Lily's godmother?"

Susanne stared at her in shock. "What?"

"I know I've only known you for a few months," Katie explained hurriedly. "But I'd like to have you as part of the family. I can't remember a lot about my mom…" Katie wiped at her eyes with the heel of her hand. "But you remind me of her a lot, and I would feel better knowing you could be there for her…" she shrugged. "Just in case."

"Just in case?"

"I've seen some of the girls fighting each other in here." Katie looked anxious. "Once or twice, I almost got stabbed by a shiv myself. I know my daddy has a lot on his plate, and I don't have any other family, so…" she met Susanne's eyes again. "Just in case."

Slowly, Susanne nodded. "I would be honored to be Lily's godmother."

Katie sighed with relief. She eyed the guard, then reached out a hand to Susanne. "I can't give you back your son. That is my burden to bear until the day I die. But if you become a part of my family, I'll do everything in my power, every day, to make you proud of me, and Lily, for the rest of your life."

How miraculous was it, that after all the years of pain and grief, Susanne's heart suddenly felt so light and warm? She looked at the young girl in front of her, earnestness and determination on her pretty face as Katie held out a hand for forgiveness. *I believe she will really do everything to uphold her promise.* Susanne thought. *How could I have hated this girl for one second?*

"You don't need to hold onto your burden anymore," Susanne said. Before the guard could object, she leaned across the table and kissed Katie on the forehead. "As far as I'm concerned, we're family now."

* * *

Susanne sat in her car, outside the prison. It seemed as if a hundred things had happened in the past few months. She'd been saved from committing suicide. She'd confronted Katie, a person she had been angry at for so long. She'd met Beth, someone she now considered a dear friend, as well as the other wonderful members of Helping Parents Heal who continued to talk with her every single day. Now she had decided to become the godmother to the daughter of the woman who had killed her son. Soon they would be family, if not by blood, certainly by paper. Susanne sighed.

She still felt the ache from the loss of Travis. But it had lightened, and she now felt more at ease. *We will always be parents; that never goes away*, Beth had said. Susanne had no doubt that there would be days where she still cried for him, but now Susanne also had friends to support her.

"What happens now?" Susanne turned to Esther, who was sitting quietly beside her.

"You have found your way to compassion and forgiveness, which was what I wanted you to do," Esther smiled. "You should be very proud of yourself for coming so far."

"But what happens after?" Susanne pressed. "Does this mean you'll be going?"

"Essentially, yes." Esther nodded. "But I'd like to remind you that our world is not as limited as you think. I will always be with you, whether you see me or not."

"But what if I *want* to see you?"

Esther smiled. "Where there is love, I will always be there. And where I am, so is love. Anything can happen, as long as love is there in your heart." And saying those words, she faded away into nothing.

* * *

Munich, Germany 1945

Esther woke to the faces of several SS men and a gun muzzle pressed to her head. She was torn, screaming, away from the bodies of her daughter and granddaughter and tossed into a transport truck headed toward Auschwitz. Her matted red hair was shaved, her ratted clothes replaced with a shapeless dress, and a number was tattooed into her arm. Esther was given a scant ration of food every day to keep her barely alive, but she barely touched it. Esther barely had the will to live, and spent her days in a trance, listlessly wandering her prison. Days, weeks passed, Esther continued to wake and exist, though every time she fell asleep, she hoped it would be her last day on earth.

She no longer prayed for anything, not even death. After all, how could anyone look down on the suffering of the people imprisoned with her and do nothing? And if there was no God, then why pray, if no one was listening?

One day, she was grabbed by one of the soldiers patrolling Auschwitz and dragged towards the gas chambers with a handful of prisoners. While the other prisoners struggled and fought, Esther went quietly. After all, life had become hell for her. Even if there was no heaven, perhaps she could still find some peace in death.

A number of soldiers, boys, barely men, were clustered in front of the death facilities, watching with amusement as the other prisoners screamed and fought their captors. They jeered and laughed, one or two throwing stones that pelted the other men and left welts.

"Stop struggling you filthy *Judea!*" one shouted.

"This is what happens when you displease the *Führer!*" another yelled.

One of the prisoners managed to escape, and he ran back toward the relative safety of camp. At an order from the leader, the boys released a pack of dogs on him. Esther tried to close out the sounds of his screams as the dogs tore him apart.

"Mama," there was a whisper at her elbow, and Esther turned to see Ilsa standing next to her, not as she had seen her last, but healthy and strong, her hair neatly combed into shinning ringlets. Instead of her BDM uniform, Ilsa was dressed in a blue frock that matched her eyes, the pattern of daisies on the dress cheerful and happy. Little Gentiana slept in her arms, looking pink and healthy.

"Ilsa," Esther whispered, suddenly unaware of the horror around her. "What are you doing here? Have I gone crazy?"

"No, Mama," Ilsa shook her head. "You're not crazy."

"But…you were dead," Esther murmured.

"This world is not as limited as you think," Ilsa smiled gently. "We are now in a place where we are safe and happy, where nothing can ever harm us."

"I should've gotten you somewhere safe sooner." Esther said sadly. The man had stopped screaming, and two soldiers dragged what was left of him toward one of the mass graves. "We might've been somewhere away from this war by now, and you would be alive and well." She looked toward the surrounding soldiers with hate. "They are responsible for your death." Ilsa's image wavered.

"Mama, it is harder to reach you when you are angry. Please, don't dwell on your hate and guilt. I am surrounded by love, and I am happy, so take comfort in that."

Esther felt tears well up in her eyes. "But they killed you, my darling."

"And I forgive them." Ilsa put out a hand to stroke Esther's cheek, and Esther felt the warmth, like a gentle breeze, caress her face. "I forgive them from the bottom of my heart."

"Why?" Esther asked, baffled.

"Because I have no wish to carry the burden of hate when I am so full of love." Ilsa touched Esther's cheek again. "Mama, I want you to forgive them, too. You have no need to hate them."

A soldier shouted at Esther and prodded her with the butt of his rifle, herding her towards the gas chambers. A ripple of laughter came from the boyish soldiers as she stumbled and fell.

"Get up." A heavy boot kicked her in the stomach and Esther doubled over in pain.

"Forgive them, Mama," Ilsa was at her side as Esther was dragged upright.

"Why should I forgive these pigs for anything?" Esther spat out loud and someone slapped her so hard her ears rang.

"You're not forgiving anyone for their sake, you're forgiving them for *your* sake. Hate is a burden," Ilsa repeated, as Esther was shoved inside the large room with the other prisoners. "You don't need to carry that with you for eternity."

"Fine. Then…" she looked into the eyes of the soldier who was holding her. "I forgive you. Even though you're killing me, I forgive you."

"Like I care," he spat in her face, and stepped back outside.

"I love you so much, Mama," Ilsa whispered encouragingly.

"Darling…I'm scared of dying," Esther whispered as the door was slammed behind her.

"It's just a quick transition," Ilsa stood in front of Esther and smiled reassuringly. The sound of gas could be heard, seeping into the room. "Just take my hand and look at me, Mama."

All around her, Esther heard the prisoners falling to their knees, choking, gasping for air as the gas slowly killed them. But Esther continued to hold her daughter's hand, and look into her eyes. When she died, and the husk that was her physical body fell to the ground, she merely felt as if she had suddenly cast off a heavy coat and was finally free. Free from the hunger, the aches and pains from the soldier's boot, and any and all feelings of anger and fear. Esther was at peace, surrounded by love that seemed to wrap her up in a warm blanket and hold her securely.

She looked down at herself. Gone was the ugly sack dress, her bony limbs, and the tattoo on her arm. Instead, her body was young and strong again, her hair flowed beautifully down to her shoulders, and she was dressed in her favorite green suit.

Esther looked briefly back at the fallen remains of her body, and saw the other prisoners had been released from their physical bodies, and were standing, whole and strong behind her.

"What is this?" Esther asked, "are we dead now?"

"Not dead, Mama. Free."

"Come with me," Ilsa said with a welcoming smile, and all the prisoners hesitantly fell in step behind her as they passed out of the gas chamber, leaving their tattered bodies behind them.

"Where are we going?" one of them asked.

"Somewhere beautiful." Ilsa answered. "Where you will live in bliss for eternity."

Chapter 9

*"Hope, for I know the plans I have for you, declares the
Lord. Plans to prosper you and not harm you. Plans to
give you hope and a future."*
Jeremiah 29:11

"Is it too festive?" Susanne muttered, turning in front of her bedroom mirror. It had been three months since Katie had asked her to be Lily's godmother, and they were finally holding a small ceremony to commemorate the occasion. It had taken a great deal of finagling, but Susanne had finally arranged for the small party to be held in one of the conjugal visiting rooms, and for a notary to be present to legalize the documents, once they were signed. She'd also brought a bag full of drinks and snacks for everyone to enjoy, and a cake with the words : "*Congratulations! It's a Godchild!*" written in frosting.

For the first time in a long time, Susanne's heart felt light. The sun shone through the window, and the trees and flowers outside seemed to be full of life and color…this was the perfect day to celebrate such a special event.

Now, if she could only decide on the best dress for the occasion… Susanne gave another turn. She loved the brightness and festivity of the red dress she was wearing, but was it too bright? Too festive? Susanne eyed the more somber, blue dress she had laid on the bed. Perhaps that would be the more appropriate dress. She didn't want to seem too excited...

"The red suits you," said a familiar voice. "There's nothing wrong with celebrating."

"Esther," Susanne smiled as she saw the beautiful woman sitting on the bed. "I thought I wasn't going to see you again."

"You didn't need me." Esther looked serene as usual. "But then again, you haven't needed me for a long time."

"So, you just came to offer fashion advice?" Susanne asked.

"No, I just wanted you to remind you of something," Esther pushed herself off the bed. "That this world is not as limited as you think, and that when you are fully in a place of love, then anything is possible." She smiled, "You are currently in a place of genuine love, Susanne. Which is why someone can finally say hello."

"Am I going to meet one of your friends?" Susanne laughed. Esther shook her head.

"Hi, Mom."

Susanne turned toward the sound of the voice she hadn't heard in two years, nine months, and two weeks.

"Travis," she whispered, and her eyes filled with tears of joy.

He looked the same as he had on the last day she'd seen him: dressed casually in a T-shirt that looked well-battered but loved, jeans, and sneakers, his light brown hair slightly mussed. Susanne felt her heart torn in two as he took a step towards her, and she smelled his special scent of deodorant and mint.

"I've been trying to reach you for so long." Travis smiled sadly, "but I couldn't get through all your hate and grief." He indicated Esther. "Thank goodness, she was able to talk to you."

"You sent Esther?" Susanne asked in surprise. She wasn't sure why she was surprised, maybe she'd just expected someone a little more… etherial. "But why? I could've joined you if you'd…let me…"

"Mom," Travis shook his head. "It was my time to go, not yours. You still have such an amazing life ahead of you, a new goddaughter, a new godson…"

Susanne stared at Travis. "I don't have a godson."

Travis winked. "Not yet."

"Don't give her too many spoilers," Esther scolded. She smiled at Susanne. "Time is fluid. And as I keep saying…"

"This world does not have as many limits as I think, I know," Susanne nodded, still feeling a little dazed.

"Look, Mom," Travis said seriously, "I want you to do something important for me. Can you do that?"

"Sure, sweetie," Susanne managed.

"I want you to stop grieving for me. No, it's time," Travis said as Susanne started to shake her head. "I was lucky enough to live a great life, I had two amazing parents who were always there for me, and I made a lot of amazing memories during my time."

"I just wished we'd had more time. And I still miss you so, so, so much," Susanne sniffed, as tears rolled down her cheeks. Travis reached out to wipe away a tear, and Susanne was aware of a slight brush, like a butterfly kiss on her face.

"I've always been here," Travis assured her. "I never left your side, not for a moment, and I'll continue to be here for you, every day of your life, for as long as you're alive." Travis took another step forward, wrapping his arms around Susanne. She was aware of a slight warmth, and though she couldn't feel his body, she felt at peace, secure in her son's embrace.

"You're going to have such an amazing life, Mom." Travis whispered. "And I want you to enjoy every minute of it. So, go live your life. Do all the things and follow all the dreams you kept putting off. Can you do that for me?"

"I'll try." Susanne sighed.

"There is no try," Travis parroted, in a perfect imitation of Yoda. "There is only do, or do not."

Susanne laughed. She couldn't help it. "Alright. I'll live the best life I can. For you."

"No, Mom," Travis rested his forehead lightly against Susanne's. "For you."

An alarm beeped on Susanne's phone. She had roughly an hour to drive to the prison for the ceremony.

"We should go," Esther said.

"I love you, Mom," Travis said, as he and Esther began to fade.

"No, don't go, I love you," Susanne wept, but as she reached out a hand, it simply passed through Travis. "Can I at least see your wings?"

Travis smiled, and for a second, Susanne saw two brilliant shafts of light sprouting from his and Esther's shoulders. A moment later, they were both gone, and the room was empty.

* * *

"Congratulations, Godmother!" Beth and Mark cheered as the notary stamped the legal document.

"I might be a little biased, but I think I have the most beautiful Goddaughter in the world," Susanne sighed as she cuddled Lily in her arms. "I might have to spoil her a little."

"Please do." Fred, Katie's father smiled as he handed slices of cake to the twins—Katie's two younger brothers, Steven and Allen. Currently, the boys were completely absorbed with their phones, but the second they realized there were sweets in their immediate vicinity, they would begin stuffing their faces. "I've got my hands full with these two."

"Well, call if you ever need a babysitter," Susanne offered. "I know how to manage young boys."

"Hey, Godmother," Katie called from her seat, "I know you're enjoying your new job, but could I hold my daughter for a moment?"

"Well, alright…" Susanne passed the drowsy infant to Katie, who was sitting next to Beth, a plate of cake on the table beside her. As she did, something fluttered to the ground, and Susanne picked it up. It was a snow-white feather, that seemed to shimmer in the light.

"What's that?" Katie asked as she rocked Lily in her arms. "Did a bird get in here?"

"No, just someone checking in on us," Susanne said, as she tucked the feather carefully in her purse. "I love you, too, Travis," she murmured under her breath, then turned her attention back to the party. She was eating good food, surrounded by new friends and family who had welcomed her into their lives. For the moment, Susanne was happy.

"Get rid of bitterness, rage, anger, harsh words and
slander as well as all types of evil behavior. Instead, be
kind to each other, tender-hearted; forgiving one another
just as God through Christ has forgiven you."
Ephesians 4:31- 4:32

Epilogue

The Impossible Place is a story about a place many of us know. It's a story about the price of unforgiveness.

There is no great equalizer for any of us who find ourselves in this place. I know I never found one.

Like many of you, I found myself awake inside an impossible place of devastation. I knew life for me would never be the same. My loss was immediately unbearable. My favorite sibling, my childhood protector had been cruelly taken from me in a heartless act. My adoring older brother who used to come in late at night and wiggle my foot to waken me, to tell me about his late-night antics was gone. We grew up chasing down the golfballs hit out of bounds to collect a quarter from the golfers. We had loved catching frogs and snakes and lizards in the woods, and Mom always supported us, allowing us to keep them around the house in "make-shift" fish tanks. We grew up poor, but carefree and happy.

When my brother was taken from me at 47, I had no offsets. Unlike Suzanne in our story, there were no counterbalancing facts that led me to be compassionate around the circumstances. His murder was impossible to comprehend and completely wrong.

After expressing for endless hours my anger and total frustration with God, I had an awakening in a moment. Self-pity and anger would not get me anything. They would not bring my brother back. I would not spend the rest of my life as a victim. I had the opportunity to turn my attention to Cliff's two beautiful children, who had just lost both parents: one dead, and the other off to prison. How was I to step into those shoes? I never had children. I had two empty bedrooms. Had God known this was coming?

Carrying unforgiveness is a poison beyond comprehension. I could not afford that death in my system. I could not allow anything that would prevent me from being my best in raising these kids. I understood what I had to do.

I surrendered. I gave in to what I knew, instead of what I felt. I need to give these teens the best life to move forward. I could not do that emotionally crippled.

I moved the teens across the country to the Dallas/Fort Worth area from the beautiful Sierra Madres in Mammoth Lakes, California. A new high school, a new town, a new life all lay ahead. Leaving behind friends and a home was a gut-wrenching reality. For all of us.

Through prayer and my letting go, I could truly love them as if I birthed them. I told them "I will raise you as if I birthed you, but you will always have one mom. When you can make peace with what she has done, I want you to go visit her in California."

All these years later, I continue to receive a Mother's Day card every May. David is in California with an awesome spouse and two beautiful little boys. Renee stayed in Texas, and is married to the love of her life, and is excelling in her career. When we step into the impossible place, we find something we might never have believed to be possible. We are never alone in that impossible place. There is a rock in that place. And love.

I am praying for every one of you who read this book. For many, our pain is indescribable and unbearable. One day, I pray that you choose to lay down your pain and anger and walk away. The pain may never totally subside as the reality of loss weighs heavy.

But the joy is greater. God, the Source, is waiting for you in that impossible place. You will find more than you require in that place.

Recently, I received a text message from my nephew, David, and I am so excited to share it with you.

Happy Mother's Day, Auntie!!
Thanks for being such an integral part of my life and such a
wonderful blessing and influential opportunity provider 🖤.

I'm sure your brother is smiling, thankful for the peace, comfort,
encouragement and support you provided for his kids to grow into
happy, thriving adults. God is good.

To be able to spend today with my family, celebrating my wife, the
mother of my two beautiful sons, is my blessing. I am very aware and
grateful for how incredibly blessed I am as a husband and a dad.

I know that I wouldn't be in this position without your amazing
God-centered influence and the love and support you poured into me.

Thank you. David

Mother's Day 2020

Their mother spent 18 years in prison, and has been released, and is living in the DFW area. I see her from time to time, and spend every holiday together. I would be lying if I said it was totally normal, but there is a new normal that works.

And my heart is so healed. That is exactly what my brother, Cliff, would want. The residual pain mostly arises when I am just sitting at graduations, sharing holidays, hosting their weddings, and all the family gatherings. I get it. I feel it. I'm okay with it.

I will always wish Cliff were here. There is a tear running down my cheek, even now, as I write this note to you. But, I know, in some way, he is smiling. One day, the door will crack open, and the light of eternity will sweep me away, and all will be made right.

I love you all.